FELON

A STORY OF DEPRAVITY AND REDEMPTION

ELLIS GEORGES

WITH
BLESSING WELLS

WARRIOR PRINCESS
NATION

Cover designed by Cafabian Heard

Published by: Warrior Publishing, a division of Warrior Princess Nation
info@warriorprincessnation.com
6435 Aliante Pkwy Ste 104-423
North Las Vegas, NV 89084

This book is dedicated to my wife, Laura, and my two children, Brittney and Christopher. Without your love and support, I would not have been able to survive what I went through. To Blessing, your presence in my life has made a tremendous difference, and for that, I am forever grateful. To my Nephew Larry Jr., I am thankful for your creativity and for bringing my words to life visually for the world to see. Lastly, I want to thank my lawyer, Mark, for defending me in my time of need. You were a God sent, and I am forever grateful. I could not have done this without you all. Thank you.

FOREWORD

G. REDMOND

As an avid reader of countless short stories and novels, I found Felon: A Story of Depravity and Redemption to be raw, unflinching, and profoundly human. From the first page to the last, Ellis's journey gripped me with a sense of urgency and emotional intensity that never let go.

To walk alongside him through the vivid, often harrowing chapters of his life was not just captivating—it was transformative. Through his words, Ellis doesn't merely recount events; he invites us into his world, exposing the pain and the hard-won pursuit of redemption with breathtaking honesty. This is not just a story—it's a reckoning and a triumph all at once.

CHAPTER 1
HAITI

The Island of Haiti was the destination God selected as my birthplace. It is a lush island located in the Caribbean, with warm tropical weather year-round and beautiful people who possess a culture rich in music, dance, and a deep respect for family relationships. As picturesque as the island may look, many of our people face challenges such as poverty and natural disasters. It is not unusual for Haitians to sacrifice everything to seek out the "American Dream." Being able to get to America meant that your family's future would be brighter, and the possibility of escaping poverty would be obtainable.

My parents didn't have much to boast about when it came to material things, but the love they had for each other was priceless. On October 24th, 1974, Sirene and Henry Georges became parents for the first time. I was their pride and joy and the physical evidence of their love. Me, a son they named Ellis, had changed their lives for the better, but the harsh reality of having another mouth to feed put a strain on them.

With little education and barely enough money to buy a plane ticket, my mother, who I fondly refer to as "Queen," along with my father, Henry, jumped at the opportunity that so many Haitians waited for and migrated to the United States on a sailboat. They risked their lives with high hopes of obtaining everything the States had to offer. Which was a better life with "Freedom and Justice for all."

I was only eleven months old when my parents made the decision to leave me behind in Haiti to be cared for by my godmother. She raised me like I was her own child until her tragic passing 8 years later. I was the tender age of eight and already dealing with the ebbs and flows of life. In Haiti, the need for family support was vital to our success and our advancement in life. After the burial of my godmother, who I loved so dearly, I would be sent to live with my "Yaya" (our name for grandma).

When my parents arrived in the States, my mother found work in a factory, while my father worked construction gigs here and there. They worked long hours and were determined to save enough money to bring me to the States to be united with them. The care and love I would receive from Yaya was the assurance they needed to stay focused and make their dream a reality.

Their family began to grow with my mother having five

more children. My sister Mulwalta was born two years after me in 1976. Three years later, my parents were blessed with twin baby boys, Johnny and Johnson. Within the next two years, they had my brother Jean and my baby sister Marlene. *Oh boy, did they have their hands full!*

My parents loved each other deeply, as well as their children. They were able to physically bond with my siblings, but for me, it was different. We bonded over the phone, having lengthy conversations. They called me every chance they had, and I fell in love with the sound of my mother's voice. The sound I knew so well from inside the womb. Yaya would report everything I was doing to them, even when I was being bad and acting out! My parents never missed a detail about my life.

My father wanted all his children to have a higher education, and it was his main purpose to risk it all and go abroad. He did not want us to be limited in what we could accomplish in life. I remember a telephone conversation with him, and he asked me what I wanted to be when I grew up. He said, "Son, what about becoming an engineer or maybe even a doctor?" He had high expectations, and since he only gave me two choices, I picked engineer. I became more and more fascinated with the idea that America was filled with endless opportunities, and the sky was the limit for me!

CHAPTER 2
REUNITED

There comes a time in life when what you wish for actually comes true. On December 19, 1993, I set foot on American soil to be reunited with my family. I was 19 years old, and so much time had passed that prior to my arrival, I couldn't stop looking at myself in the mirror. I wanted to impress my parents, so I took extra time working on my appearance and grooming myself. I wanted Queen and my dad to be proud of their firstborn child. I wanted my siblings to think highly of me as well. After all, I was the big brother. We spent years having phone conversations to keep our connections strong, but that would no longer have to be the case for us.

The taxi ride from the airport to my new home was surreal. My eyes were opened so wide, and I was taking in the scenery like a kid going to Disney World for the first time. I looked forward to seeing beautiful mansions lined along the beach and everyone living like the "Rich and Famous." So many thoughts were running through my mind, and my heart was beating so fast with anticipation. However, as we got closer to the address, the scenery wasn't as promising. For a moment, I thought to myself that I might want to go back home! The saying is true: there's a hood in every city, and that's just where my parents resided. I quickly dismissed that thought because nothing mattered more than what was about to transpire.

As the taxi slowly approached the house, I could see my brother Johnny waiting outside. The taxi came to a complete stop, and I leaped out of the car to grab my bags from the trunk. Johnny ran up to me, shaking my hand and giving me the warmest welcome I'd ever received. He took my suitcase and motioned for me to go inside the house, where the others were waiting.

As I entered the house, Johnson, who is the shy brother, looked at me and quickly put his head down. I reached my hand out for a handshake to ease the awkwardness. Once we shook hands, the energy changed. Johnson had a huge smile on his face! I knew he was just as excited as I was because a close friend of his had called me weeks earlier to tell me that Johnson couldn't stop talking about meeting his big brother Ellis.

I was reunited with my family that day, surrounded by my closest relatives and my parents, who gave me life. A void in me was filled as it felt good to see the similarities in our appearance and mannerisms.

My philosophy professor once said, *"**Family and friends are like hidden treasures, seek them out and enjoy their riches.**"* I had a lot of bonding to do with them and a lot to learn about my new environment.

CHAPTER 3
MY LIFE

I knew very little English when I arrived, and I didn't have a high school diploma from my schooling in Haiti. I had to enroll in Miami Edison Senior High School. Most 19-year-olds had already completed high school and were ready to start college. After meeting with the school counselor, I was told I had to repeat the twelfth grade. I knew deep inside that I would struggle to get A's because of the language barrier, so I requested to be placed along with the Juniors. It didn't bother me one bit because I would be attending high school with three of my siblings, Johnny, Johnson, and my sister Mulwalta. She was always by my side, laughing and enjoying being around her eldest sibling. I prayed for this experience, and it was happening.

It was like clockwork in our house during the week. I remember Queen waking up at four in the morning to go to work in the factory. She would work hard six days a week. On paydays, Queen would gather us together to give us our bus fare so we could get back and forth to school. She gave me, Mulwalta, and the twins ten dollars each. The younger siblings were handed five dollars each. She did the best she could with the little that was left over. Her bi-weekly earnings totaled around six hundred dollars, and with my father out of work due to an on-the-job injury, he had little to no income. Things were better than what I was accustomed to, but not by much. My mother would always drop wisdom on us as she distributed her hard-earned money. I can still hear Queen's voice telling us in Creole, ***"Pa konpare tèt ou ak lòt moun, paske konparezon se vòlè jwa."*** That means do not compare yourself to others, for comparison is the thief of joy. I held on dearly to those words.

My mother was a pure, genuine soul. She worked tirelessly outside and inside the home and made it look easy. She was a great cook and nurtured us while teaching us the facts of life. I often wondered how she managed it all. I knew her lifestyle was burdensome, but she never held back from giving God all the praise, and she kept her faith in Him.

I didn't come to this country with much. It wasn't like I left a lot of stuff behind by choice; I didn't have a huge selection of clothes and shoes. I remember getting ready for school, and my brother Johnny would hook me up with his clothes to wear while his twin Johnson was pushing my foot in a pair of Nike sneakers so I could step my swagger up! I was in desperate need of a makeover. "I am in America now!" I thought to myself. Time to dress like a Yankee! I was thankful for what they did; however, I knew as a man, I wanted to be able to hold my own and contribute to the household and alleviate some of the burden from my parents.

After graduating high school, my father wanted to send me to NYU to study engineering. We began to calculate the college expenses, but it was a no-go for me. What I wanted versus my reality were two different things. I knew I had to work because my family needed the money, and the only way to keep up with the bills was to do just that. I took a job at a meat market, making $5.25 per hour. The pay I was receiving helped some, but it wasn't going to make enough of a difference to see a significant improvement in our circumstances. Higher education was going to be my ticket to a brighter future. I enrolled at Miami Lakes Technical School and completed 1500 hours in Electronics Technology. I earned a trade certification, and I figured this would be a short-term solution to my current problem.

CHAPTER 4

MON CHERI

The year was 1996, and I was now twenty-two years old and employed at Publix Supermarket. I was hired to stock groceries. I wanted the cashier position because it paid more, but I understood I would have to be patient and work my way up. Let my father tell it, there were no such things as shortcuts. You had to earn your position.

At that time, Publix was paying more than my previous job, and I was having a lot of fun there. It was pretty cool meeting new people and working with the public. I would wake up daily with a positive attitude and take pride in my work. It is how I was raised.

After weeks of being at Publix, I grew very fond of a co-worker. Her name was Laura. I had feelings for her that I had never felt before. She was beautiful and curvy and just my type of woman. Laura was fine! I wanted her to be **Mon Cheri**. "My sweetheart." It was time to put my romantic skills to the test. I was a very confident man. I knew God blessed me with good looks, and from what I was learning, most women loved a man who fit the description: tall, dark, and handsome. I felt strongly about my chances with Laura.

It was business as usual at work, and I spotted her in the employee break room using a pay phone. I mustered up the courage to walk over to her and ask if I could interrupt her phone conversation to ask her something. She must've known I was plotting to ask her out because her exact words were, "I have a boyfriend." Sheesh! This girl just shut me down! That experience made me try even harder to get her to like me. My philosophy is that if you try hard enough, you will eventually have what you want, and I wanted Laura.

So many different ideas were playing out in my head about how to get her to give me a moment of her time. The thought of writing her a love letter entered my mind; I was sure that would do the trick. The night before work, I stayed up late to make sure the letter was perfect. When I presented it to her the following afternoon, she told me to take it back! She didn't even take a second to read it. I got shut down once again! This lady was one of a kind. It made me even more attracted to her. I decided to fall back and just observe her for a while. Finally, I figured out why I wasn't getting anywhere with Laura. She was a no-nonsense type of woman when she was on the clock.

Laura was a stellar employee who had no time for games.

My buddies Max and Waiguy would joke around at work to make the day go by faster, but there was no joking with Laura! The three of us really had a pretty cool bond with each other. Trying to get Laura to soften up would be a challenge. Laura was the only Black woman I knew that when she spoke, she sounded like a white girl. While having a conversation with her, I just had to ask why she didn't sound like the other Black girls I knew. She said, "Listen, Ellis, I can speak three different languages: Professional, Patois (a Jamaican dialect), and even Hood!" So, depending on her audience, she didn't want to be misunderstood. She mentioned that things were easier that way. I still didn't understand her theory then, but later I would.

I was so captivated by her beauty, but extremely impressed with how intelligent she was. In my private thoughts and prayers, it was my desire to settle down with a woman who possessed both. I couldn't mess this up. I really wanted to show her that I was serious about taking things further. Five months later, we were dating steadily. My patience had finally paid off! I had someone in my life that I could care for, provide, and show unconditional love to. But God placed her in my life because I would need her shoulder to cry on and be there for me through my trials. In 1997, my Queen was diagnosed with breast cancer, and the news devastated my family. In a flash, I went from feeling like the man to feeling so helpless. To prolong my mother's life, she underwent surgery to remove the cancer. Laura had my back through this entire ordeal. We ended up moving into our own apartment. Together, we helped Queen through her recovery.

CHAPTER 5
LOVE AND HAPPINESS

L ife's roller coaster had taken me on a lot of ups and downs, but emotionally, I felt renewed again. Queen was healthy again, and I enjoyed spending as much time as I could with Mon Cheri. It was so beautiful to watch the relationship between her and my mother blossom. Both Laura and my mother were excellent cooks, and I was reaping the benefits. Laura cooked the best brown stew chicken with rice and peas, and could curry the best chicken I've ever tasted. I had found my soulmate, my future wife, and my belly bulging out from eating so much.

In June of 1999, we welcomed our baby girl, Brittney, to the world, and were married a year later, on August 27, 2000. I didn't know I could feel loved on a deeper level until I held my baby girl. Two years after that, Laura gave birth to our son Christopher, who would complete our family. Although my wife wanted to have three children, she felt complete with her boy and girl, and so did I. Brittney and Christopher were my everything; they each had such unique personalities, and watching Laura nurture our children was the best part of it all. She was natural at it and made it look so easy. I've always heard people talk about how time flies when you're having fun, and in the short span of 6 years, Laura and I were married and raising a family. What more can a man dream of?

It was our desire to ensure our children had the best life that we could afford to give them. I remember my wife tossing around the idea of buying a home. She ran down the pros and cons of being a homeowner vs. a renter. At the time, we were renting an apartment in Broward County, Florida. Since we were both happy there, we made a clear decision to work and save enough money to buy our first home there. With Mon Cheri by my side, anything was possible. She worked two jobs, and her accounting skills were impeccable. She managed all the finances in our household. However, with the children, it became a challenge to juggle everything she had going on. Shortly after Christopher was born, Laura's grandmother moved from New York to help us care for our children, which really allowed us to work longer hours and work towards our dream of homeownership.

I was so happy with the direction of my life, and being a father and husband felt incredible. Queen enjoyed being a grandmother and showed Brittney and Christopher so much love and affection. Sometimes, I would watch her interact with my children, and I would imagine it being me being nurtured by her. It was a fantasy I've played out in my mind that I've always kept to myself. I was extremely fortunate that my kids could experience love from both of their grandmothers.

It was about three years of working our asses off and being diligent with our savings that we were able to sign a contract and put a down payment on a spacious townhome that was selling for $350k. I was so relieved that our sacrifices were finally paying off. It felt like forever trying to get to this point, and I prayed so hard that everything would go smoothly.

The word began to spread about Laura and me waiting to close on a house. While sharing the news with her daughter (Laura's aunt), Laura's grandmother informed her that they could save $100k if they would consider moving to Miami-Dade County in the south end of Florida. I wasn't too keen on the idea at all. I mean, I loved the sound of saving money, but I also loved my lifestyle living in Broward County. I was comfortable there as it wasn't easy for me to just relocate and start over. Laura had begun building her business, and her clientele was growing. I felt it would be very risky for us to move. I was feeling the stress coming down on me, so Laura suggested we take a weekend with the family to check out this new development her aunt was raving about. We loaded the car with our kids and grandmother. We headed to Southwest Miami, about a forty-five-minute drive from Broward.

We spent the day with Laura's aunt, touring model homes that had larger floor plans and more options than the townhome we put our money down on. I could see the excitement on Laura's face as she walked through the rooms, imagining what she would do with the space and envisioning Brittney and Christopher playing in the backyard. It was true that we could have a bigger house for much less in that area. Laura and her grandma would be only minutes away from other family members, and that made our decision easy.

I reminded my wife that if this was what she truly desired, we would have to act fast. The housing prices were rising rapidly, and we needed to get our money back and cancel our contract with the Realtor in Broward. I personally wanted to provide a comfortable home for my family and my wife's grandmother to live in. Either way, it was time to upgrade, whether we stayed in Broward or relocated to Miami. I would do anything to ensure the future success of my children, even if it meant starting over. I remember the sacrifice my parents made so I could be granted this opportunity to give my family more than what they ever had.

In May 2005, we were jingling the keys to our beautiful four-bedroom home in S.W. Miami with enough space for all of us and a dog! I was living the American Dream. My friends and family were so proud of us and wondered how we did it. They looked up to us for advice, and I told them Laura would steer them in the right direction. She was like a walking encyclopedia filled with so much knowledge. She'd spend time with people, helping them map out their goals and sharing some of the helpful tips she learned along the way during the home-buying process.

We were getting acclimated to our new home, and I embraced my new neighborhood and actually loved being closer to the ocean. Our community was growing fast as construction continued, and more people were moving in.

It was four years in; Brittney was already ten, and little Christopher was seven. They were very bright students, and they got along well with each other. Each day, we did what most parents do: get up, get the kids ready for school, go to work, pick up the kids, eat dinner, and go to bed, then repeat. It was very tiring, but seeing them smile and keeping them safe was my duty. A feeling I was most proud of.

That same year, my mother's cancer returned, but this time, it attacked her ovaries. She had been cancer-free for twelve years, and I never fathomed going down this road again. The cancer was so aggressive that it was only months later that she lost her battle.

Queen passed away the day after Valentine's Day on February 15, 2010. I was empty. It felt like my heart was ripped right out of my chest. I sobbed for a long time, and I just knew this was the worst thing that could have ever happened to me until this very tragic day, ten years later, April 24, 2020. My life was forever changed.

CHAPTER 6

DREADFUL DAY

It was now April 2020, and the world as we knew it had completely shut down, and everyone was quarantined in their homes because of COVID-19. With so much uncertainty over what would happen next, I was shaken to my core. I felt like we were living in the end of days. It was overwhelming watching the news and learning how many people died overnight from COVID-19. The virus was spreading rapidly, and neither scientists nor the government could offer concrete plans to stop it.

I was furloughed from my job at Encore, which was an audio-visual company. I later had to apply for unemployment and went weeks without any pay. Laura began working remotely and set up an office in our home. Things were quite crazy for her, and just like so many other people working remotely, this transition was sudden and challenging. Laura worked in IT and was responsible for so many additional tasks when this happened. Thankfully, at this time, Brittney had already graduated from high school; Chris was in his junior year and began learning remotely.

We were all together, safe in our home, trying to survive this pandemic. Praying our way through and getting closer to God was all we could do, just in case the worst happened.

It was the morning of April 24, 2020, at 5:30 am, to be precise, when Brittney was moving about the house and grabbed her keys to retrieve some items out of her car. In no time, she was back in the house and told me she was having trouble with the lock on her car door. It was still early, and I couldn't quite understand what she was trying to express. She looked at me and said, "Daddy, I think my car was broken into!" My wife and I couldn't believe what she was telling us! We owned three vehicles, and two of those vehicles were parked in the driveway, with the third car parked in front of the house. Brittney and I checked the cameras, with our eyes bulging out desperately trying to make out who this guy was! He stole two pairs of Nike tennis shoes, sunglasses, keys, and some cash that my daughter kept in her car. Quite naturally, I felt inclined to check to see if the other cars had been tampered with. To my surprise, my vehicle, which was a Honda Accord parked right next to hers, had been broken into as well. Laura's black Mercedes was parked in front of the house, untouched.

Instinctively, I rushed to my glove box and prayed that when I opened it, my handgun would still be there. My breath left my body because what had started as a bad morning just got a whole lot worse; the gun had been stolen. It was a Pandemic happening, for Christ's sake. Who would do this to us, and why? What would happen to my gun in the hands of a criminal? So many thoughts and questions were running through my mind.

I called 911 and waited for the police to arrive at our home. After waiting about 30 to 45 minutes, an unmarked car pulled up, and two male detectives approached our door. Both detectives looked to be of Hispanic heritage. They followed the usual routine of asking questions and taking a report of what happened. I kept as calm as possible so that my family wouldn't fret, but honestly, I felt violated and extremely uneasy about the whole ordeal.

I gave them the suspect's description, and they also retrieved a copy of the footage from the Ring Camera. A white male wearing a black hospital mask, black shorts, and a dark pair of tennis shoes, and to prevent leaving his fingerprints behind, he was wearing black latex gloves. He was up to no good, and it was clear he had bad intentions.

I was trying to look at the bright side of things and say to myself, "Well, at least he didn't steal the cars. Or at least he didn't break into our home." It helped ease my mind some, but not totally. We went on about our day, but I didn't get any rest that night. How could I? It was my first time being a victim of a robbery, and with my handgun being stolen, I did not feel safe. I slept with my rifle out like any man of the household would.

CHAPTER 7
THE RETURN

It was around 5 am when I was startled out of my sleep. Our dog Rambo was barking so aggressively that I felt something was wrong. This behavior was unusual for Rambo, especially at this time of morning.

I grabbed my rifle and peered out of my front window, and wouldn't you know, he was back wearing the same f*%king thing from the morning before! Our eyes locked in on each other, so we instantly went into defense mode. He jetted off because he knew that he was caught dead in the act of committing a crime. I felt a rush of adrenaline running through my body as I was experiencing fear, along with my instincts telling me to protect myself.

My wife was still asleep, so I yelled for Brittney to call 911. I grabbed my car keys to follow the suspect so he wouldn't get away. This guy was a criminal who was set on stealing from us, and with my gun in his possession, maybe he would even kill us! A person like this shouldn't be on the loose. Who was this guy?

I watched his every move as he ran to the back of my neighbor's house, the block behind us on 107th Avenue, where he parked his scooter or, should I say, his "getaway" ride. He started it up and, in no time, peeled off down the street, forcing me to pick up just a little speed to keep track of him. He was heading towards a dead-end construction zone less than a mile away from our home on S.W. 232nd Street. We were moving parallel to each other, and he was on my right side. We were nearing the dead end, where two concrete barriers were placed to close off the road. This guy was so desperate to get away that he dashed right in front of me, attempting to squeeze through the narrow gap between the two barriers. His miscalculation sent him plowing into the right barrier, causing me to swerve and impact the left barrier.

I was shaken up a bit after hitting the concrete wall, but I had to think quickly because my life was in jeopardy. I couldn't determine the suspect's whereabouts, plus it was still very dark at the time, and with the absence of streetlights, it was difficult to see. I left the house in such a hurry and left my damn cell phone, so I couldn't call 911. I threw the car in reverse and decided to head back home and wait for the police to arrive. I was driving south on 107th Avenue, and I saw police cars speeding past me with their sirens blaring, heading in the direction of my home. I was relieved knowing that Brittney got the call through and that the police were responding.

If I can remember correctly, it was about 5 Miami-Dade Police cars in front of my home when I pulled up. Flashing lights lit up my block like it was Christmas. I had no choice but to park my car by the mailbox a few feet away from my front yard. As I began to exit my vehicle, I was approached by an officer who had a perplexed look on his face. His eyebrows were scrunched together when he said, "Didn't I pass you down the road back there?" I said, "Yes, that was me," while nodding my head up and down.

Then he noticed the front end of my vehicle and asked, "What happened to your vehicle?" "I see some damage to your front end." I took a few steps and stood next to him, facing the front end of the car. I explained to the officer that I was following the guy who tried to break into my home and that I hit the barrier. I pointed in the direction of S.W. 232nd St, where the accident took place.

He took out his flashlight, shone the light in the front passenger window, and saw my rifle on the front seat. I didn't want any problems, so I quickly explained to the officer that I was licensed to carry. He whistled to his partner for him to come over to the vehicle. He proceeded to ask me if I had a safe for it, and I told him no. I mentioned that I did have a bag for it inside the house because I knew about the importance of gun safety. His partner made it over to us, removed the rifle from the front seat, and immediately checked the chamber. When he saw the bullet in the chamber, he removed it and kept my rifle in his possession. A lot was happening around me, with multiple conversations taking place simultaneously, making it difficult for me to process it all. I saw my wife explaining to one officer about the cars being broken into the previous day. I could see the panic on her face as she expressed to the officer how hysterical she was when Brittney told her the horrific news. She was still in her moo-moo, (nightgown), and I hated that she had to be awakened this way.

As I looked around, I realized my wife's car was gone, and I didn't see Chris outside. I thought to myself, "holy shit" where is my wife's car, and where is my son? My head was spinning.

Laura said she sent Chris to search for me because when she called my cell phone, it started ringing on the kitchen counter where I had left it. I could kick myself for leaving my phone. I also looked around to see if the two detectives from Friday morning's burglary were there, but unfortunately, they were nowhere in sight. I would have felt more comfortable with them on the scene since they already knew our situation. I noticed a set of headlights coming down the block, and once I could see the body of the car, I knew it was Chris. Thank God he had made it back okay. I could remember feeling my chest loosen up some, allowing me to breathe a little deeper. I kept telling myself to try to remain calm, but my heart rate was still elevated.

Things started to progress with the same officer asking for my driver's license and registration. I cooperated, went inside to get my wallet, and grabbed my registration from the car. As I handed it over, the officer stepped away to talk privately on his cell phone.

Approximately 15 minutes went by when he made his way over to me again and said, "Georges, I'm going to detain you. However, you are not under arrest." I could tell by the look in his eyes that he needed to cuff me. I understood the drill, so I placed my hands behind my back as the officer slapped the cuffs on me. The sound of the cuffs tightening around my wrist and the sound of the keys turning the lock still haunts me to this day. This was a first for me, and instantly, I felt my freedom being stripped away. The officer escorted me to the back of his police car, just like I've seen a million times in the movies. Only this time, it was NOT a movie. It was happening to me in real life; there was no take one and no director shouting "Action."

CHAPTER 8
SHIFT CHANGE

The police presence was growing as more and more cop cars lined my entire block. I could see the neighbors standing in front of their homes, looking intently, trying to figure out what the hell was going on. It was around 7:25 am that I was informed that a shift change was happening. The officer said I would be placed in another squad car, and the investigation would continue with the other officers who had just come on duty. I was ok with that because I couldn't wait to breathe in some fresh air and get a chance to stretch my legs. I looked down towards the ground and noticed that I was still in my Long Johns and a white T-shirt. I was shaking my head because no one outside of my family ever saw me dressed this way. It was a short walk to the other squad car, but it felt so awkward walking with my hands cuffed behind my back. The sun finally rose, and the temperature was growing warmer and warmer by the second. I turned my head in the direction of my wife and kids and gave them a look that meant to stay strong. I was praying that this would all be over soon.

But shit changed when the shift changed. I had just learned that the "Bad Guy," the suspect, lost his life. Now, this was a full-on investigation and the absolute worst day of my life. I was handled by two officers whom I will refer to as "RoboCop" and "Frankenstein." Their demeanor reeked of arrogance, and their negative judgment of me was evident in the way they dealt with me. (You'll learn more about that later.)

It had just occurred to me that the previous officer from the 1st shift still had my personal information, so I simply asked Officer Frankenstein to retrieve my wallet and release it to my wife. His response was, "How much money is your wallet?" I don't know if this was proper protocol, but this didn't seem right, and I knew for sure that his tone wasn't right. Needless to say, they kept my wallet in their possession, along with the keys to my car and my rifle. I thought to myself, why is everyone taking from me?

I could still feel the disgust that he had towards me as "RoboCop" slammed the car door and walked away. I was left in the back of the squad car in so much discomfort, and being caged in like that caused me anxiety.

My mind took me back to a time when Queen told me a story when I was a kid. She said my great-grandfather gave me a necklace to wear, but after days of wearing it, I told her

I wanted it off. She said I would tug at it and rub my neck because I hated the way it felt on me. She giggled a bit when she recalled that I told her, "I just wanted to be free."

Now, with my hands cuffed behind me, the feeling was back but magnified a thousand times. I felt humiliated, and the need to break free was bringing on emotions of fear and terror. The temperature in the car was heating up along with the temperature outside.

Hours had gone by, and I was left in the car with the windows rolled up all the way. Not even cracked a little for the air to circulate. The car was off, and with no AC running, it was becoming difficult to breathe. We were in South Miami, Florida, for Christ's sake, and I was hot as hell!

I was trying to be patient, but after three hours of neglect, I started to panic. I raised my voice for someone to help me, but obviously, with the windows rolled up, I had to literally scream. I shouted as loud as I could, "Can somebody open the window, please?" I said this repeatedly and exerted so much energy to get help, but no one came to my rescue.

I was violated and abused that day. Not even a dog gets left in the car without the AC on, and here I was, a human being, getting treated inhumanely.

I cannot ignore the fact that I knew I was being racially profiled. I've heard countless testimonies of black men who have been mistreated by the police because they were being judged by their skin color.

My wife told the detective that I badly needed some air and water. The detective granted her request, so Chris went into the house and returned to the squad car, holding a cold bottle of water in his hand. The detective opened the car door for me to get out and uncuffed me so I could have a drink. I guzzled down the water so fast that the plastic bottle crumbled in my hand! After quenching my thirst, I noticed a crime scene van pulling up in front of my home. I was only free from the cuffs for two minutes before they were slapped back on my wrist. I was told that the crime scene investigators were there to take photos of me and the car. Seven hours had passed since the ordeal began, and I doubted if I could take much more of this.

The detective told Laura that he had to take me in for questioning, and she threw her hands up and said, "What am I supposed to do now?" He took a deep breath before responding and said, "If you were my wife, I would get a lawyer." He even gestured for her to say whatever she had on her mind before they took me in. I guess from his experience, he knew that it would get ugly from this point. Or maybe from his experience, he knew this could be the final moment where most black men would never return home. She walked over to me and hugged me so tightly. She whispered in my ear, "I'm going to get you the best lawyer." "Don't worry, Ellis, I got you." I could feel the strength of her hug and the tone of her voice, which showed that she meant every word.

Laura looked me over and wanted to make sure I had nothing of value on me. When her eyes glanced down at my hand, she said, "Ellis, take off your ring." I looked down at my finger, hesitant to remove my wedding band. It became a part of me after all these years. I never took my ring off since the wedding. Laura explained that if I didn't remove it now, they would make me take it off later. She was right; they already had my personal belongings.

I sucked my teeth and started tugging at the ring while trying to twist it off. The ring must have been fighting back to stay on because it wouldn't budge. Laura sent Chris back into the house to get some dishwashing liquid and water to give it some slippage. After a few tugs and wiggling my finger back and forth, it was finally off. The struggle was over. I massaged my hand to get the blood circulating again. I looked down at the tan line on my ring finger, which made my heart sink. At that moment, I felt like I had just been stripped of the most important thing: Laura and my family.

It was about a twenty-minute drive from my home to the police department. I stared out the window as the squad car traveled down the block. I took one last look at all the chaos happening in front of my home, and that image is one I will never forget. I could see the neighbors' eyes trailing me as the cop car crept out of the neighborhood.

I rested my head against the seat and inhaled deeply to get some air in my lungs. On the exhalation, I realized I hadn't eaten all day! I was feeling even weaker because of it. But surviving this ordeal was the only thing on my mind, along with trying to wrap my head around who the hell the "Bad Guy" was and why he chose to return.

CHAPTER 9
THE SUSPECT

According to the West Palm Beach Public Record, the "Bad Guy", aka "BG," spent most of his youth in and out of jail. The "BG" was a White male, age 35, with multiple arrests for felony battery, trespassing, fraud, and grand theft. He was a career criminal who was no stranger to illegal activities and had a record that stemmed all the way back to 2007.

It was reported in the Palm Beach Daily News that on March 27, 2014, he and another individual were charged with selling fake jewelry to Avenue Jewelers. It was reported that the owner of the jewelry store notified police about the illegal transaction, and together, they set up a sting operation to lure them back to the store. "BG" returned with the intention of profiting $8,000 from the sale of the fake jewelry. To their surprise, they walked right into the trap set by the police, which resulted in both men being arrested for grand theft and the "BG" being charged with two counts of fraud. There is a strong comparison here, and if my thought process is correct, Mr. "BG" was always looking to return for more.

Now, here I am, trying to figure out how the hell I ended up in cuffs with my life at the mercy of the police. Was it truly because of my actions or the color of my skin? My answer is the latter. It became evident to me that if I put up any resistance to being handcuffed, I would end up just like the brothers who suffered brutal beatings or even death by the police. The 2nd shift officers made it known that they were the law around here. They abused their power and treated me like shit.

I knew I had to be smart about it and defend my rights the legal way. I made a promise to myself that I would file a formal complaint with the Bureau as soon as this was over.

I couldn't help but think of all the Black civil rights leaders who fought so hard, even to their deaths, for equal rights. I was reminded of the great Marcus Garvey, who, in his writings, said, "You have reached the point where the victory is to be won from within and can only be lost from within." I was having a pep talk with myself to keep my emotions together. I mumbled repeatedly, "I will overcome this tribulation." "I will overcome this tribulation."

We finally arrived at MDPD, and I was taken to an interrogation room. Once inside the room, the detective uncuffed me, and I could begin to feel the blood circulate through my hands again. I rubbed both of my wrists to help soothe the discomfort. I tried to do some deep breathing to release some tension and stay focused. The room looked no different than the crime shows I'd seen on TV. It was a small room with a table and three chairs. It must have been an hour and a half that had gone by as I sat freezing my behind off. The room was ice cold, and at times, I tucked my arms inside my shirt to bring up my body temperature. It was moments after that that Robocop finally entered the room again. I couldn't stand to see him coming. He nonchalantly asked if I was hungry and if I wanted something to eat. He even made a suggestion and asked if I wanted pizza. I was totally taken aback by his question. In my mind, I thought you must be kidding me! I didn't want any food; I wanted to go home! After turning down the food, he asked if I needed to go to the bathroom. That was a quick yes for me. I stood up from the chair, ready to get out of the room. He escorted me to the restroom, waited at the door until I was done, and then escorted me back to the interrogation room.

In my entire adult life, I've never been watched like this before. Having an officer wait for you on the other side of the bathroom door made me feel so uncomfortable. My gut was telling me that I was in for a long night as the vibes I was getting from Robocop continued to be ill.

I needed to check in with my wife. I silently prayed that she and the kids were holding up ok. I waited back in the room for another few hours without any updates from anyone. My mind couldn't stop replaying the events I experienced within the last 24 hours. The disgust and frustration I felt every time I thought about how I was treated by the 2nd shift officers spiked my heart rate. Everything about my situation was so unjust. I was the one robbed, my gun was stolen, I was targeted again the next morning, I struggled to breathe, I begged for water, and was handcuffed in the back of a car for hours. I've read about the oppression of black men in America, and through the stories told, I felt the pain they went through. On that dreadful day, every inch of my body physically felt the pain and oppression.

Internally, I wanted to handle my own affairs and get my own representation, but I was not in control of my life anymore. This realization was hard to accept, and as a Black man facing interrogation, this reality was downright horrifying. As I mentioned before, Laura is a strong woman, and procrastination wasn't in her vocabulary. I knew she was doing all the necessary legwork to get me the best legal representation. She was the master thinker for our family, so I had to trust the process.

Finally, Robocop entered the room, holding some papers in his hand. He sat in the chair across from me, slapped the papers on the table, and told me that he needed me to sign some documents. I found that strange because I thought I would be asked questions about the incident. The first thing that came out of my mouth was, "First of all, you haven't even told me why I'm here." His response will forever be in my memory bank when he replies, "Mr. Georges, you're being charged with homicide."

The human body can experience a wide range of emotions. However, there isn't a word that can describe exactly what I felt at that moment. I tried to swallow the lump that was forming in my throat, and by my own volition, I told the officer that I wanted my lawyer present. With that being said, there was nothing else for Robocop to do but proceed to tell me that I would be transferred to Turner Gilford Knight Correctional Center and charged with the death of the "BG."

CHAPTER 10
GOD BE WITH ME

How was this happening to me? I pleaded with God for his presence to be with me. I was in my darkest hour and at my lowest point. I had to go through what I was experiencing all by myself. It was me against the world.

The internal struggle that was going on inside my head was causing torment in my mind. I battled to think positively, but defeat and the will to give up were winning. I had to dig deep within myself and earnestly pray for God to rescue me.

We were coming up on NW 41st St, where TGK was located. I stared at the building and noticed how intimidating the concrete structure was. Its true design was to ensure no escape, and without much sunlight filtering through, it would be enough punishment for any human being. What's a jail without barbed wire surrounding the building? TGK lacked none of the extra security features. I never fathomed a day like this would be my fate, as I was only trying to protect my family from this criminal. My heart rate increased with every step; one could only imagine what awaited me on the inside.

Being stripped of my dignity and respect was what awaited me. K41257 was my inmate number, or should I say, "Slave Code." I remember one of the corrections officers saying to his peers I'll never spend another birthday with my family again. That shit was messed up! He had some nerve to make light of my situation when I haven't even had my day in court.

I was stripped down to nothing and made to bend over and cough to prove I didn't have anything stuffed up my ass. I had to trade my long johns for the orange jumpsuit the inmates wore. The ridicule I experienced was beyond describable. But it wasn't until I was hit with the double whammy that made me want to shit my pants. I had just learned that I was being charged with 2nd-degree murder with "No Bond." If my mother were alive, she would interlock her hands together, look up to the sky, and holler, "JESUS CHRIST!"

This situation was literally the scariest moment of my life. I was confined to a holding cell with strangers and felt unsure of my future. Everywhere I looked, I couldn't help but see Black or Brown people taking up space in the holding tank. It was about fifty men, some with their heads down contemplating their fate, while others looked disheveled or high off some drugs or something.

Where were the white criminals? I know firsthand that they are out there. Do police officers heavily patrol minority groups vs. whites? Hell yeah, they do!! In the US, African Americans are historically more likely to be incarcerated than any other race or ethnic group. I'm living proof and a living testament that biased law enforcement practices and racism still exist in this country.

I would be remiss if I didn't say that I thought about the suspect, who was now deceased. I felt horrible because it was not my intention for this to happen, not to myself or anyone else, as a matter of fact. I know I'm strong because the heaviness of the past 36 hours would break anyone. "I will overcome this tribulation," continued to echo throughout my entire soul. It was around 6 p.m. when my name was called to be taken up to a cell. I was in their control now, and I felt like a slave, made to obey. My feet were moving forward, but I wanted to get the hell out of there. Was the officer right about me never going home? How can I be charged with 2nd-degree murder if the police didn't have all the facts?

I'm an educated man. I've studied the Bible, philosophical material, and even poetry by the great Black poets. I'm so thankful for Maya Angelou's quote, "You may encounter many defeats, but you must not be defeated. In fact, it may be necessary to encounter the defeats so you can know who you are, what you can rise from, how you can still come out of it." Her words were so powerful and refueled me just enough to keep me from suffering a mental breakdown. With my life in jeopardy, and the mere thought of never being with my family again, was all the motivation I needed to stay focused.

We came to a stop, and the guard stopped at my cell. Cell number 215, to be exact. Its dimensions were 6X8 with a flimsy cot and a sink and toilet in the back left corner. I stepped into the cell, turned around to face the officer, and watched as he turned the key. But that jail cell door did not lock. Even when the officer thought it was secured, it wasn't. Cell 215 was open. You can't tell me that God isn't real. I knew His presence was with me, and this was just the sign I needed from the Father. I continued to pray throughout the night as my bond hearing was scheduled for the next morning. There was still no communication from Laura, and I didn't know if I would even have legal representation. Would the Judge "see me for the good man I was, or would the Judge see me as a criminal? I would find out in the next few hours what would happen next in my life.

My original hearing time of 9 a.m. got pushed back to noon. I was already sleep-deprived and so hungry that I felt a headache coming on. I could hear Laura, with her sarcasm, saying, "You should've eaten the pizza!"

With COVID-19 changing the way the courts operated, the inmates who were waiting for their hearing were not allowed in the courtroom. Because of the mandates, not even family or friends of the inmates could be present. They were given links to join a Zoom call to listen to what was happening. Everything was done by video streaming.

I didn't know I had an attorney sitting in the actual courtroom until my case was called. He was not just any Attorney but "The Beast," one of Miami's highly respected defense attorneys. I saw The Beast on the screen as he stood up to introduce himself and asked permission to speak on my behalf. I was rejoicing on the inside as this was truly the breakthrough I needed. I had to contain my excitement, so I shook my head and responded with a "yes." He was a white male, probably in his mid-50s, wearing a dark-colored suit with a navy-blue tie and a white and blue plaid shirt. Everyone, including myself, wore the blue mask, so I couldn't make out exactly what he looked like. All I saw was his dark hair and that he wore glasses. At the time, nothing mattered more than knowing Laura had managed to keep it together to make this happen. He was the only Attorney present in the courtroom. I knew that God was with me. He also mentioned that about ninety of my family, friends, and loved ones were on the Zoom call supporting me. That information alone warmed my heart, and I could feel a sense of relief.

On the bench sat a white female Judge wearing the typical black robe. She appeared to be young, and the court clerks and prosecutors seated below her shuffled through papers and watched the monitors.

While watching the screen, I noticed a rectangular wooden plaque hung on the wall behind the Judge. Its quote read, "We Who Labor Here Seek Only The Truth."

I prayed for this to be true for me. I prayed that the Judge would see me as a man and not judge me by the color of my skin. The truth is all I wanted to be revealed. Thank God I had The Beast on my side. What happened next was nothing but a miracle.

After The Beast got through with his attorney's jargon, the Judge granted the motion for me to be released on house arrest. Oh my God! With sweat dripping off my forehead, I just wanted to fall on my knees and thank God for allowing the Judge to find favor with me right then and there. But what I will never forget was the look on that nasty correction officer's face when I realized that he had stuck his foot in his mouth. He said I'll never be with my family again. I was the 1st man in the state of Florida to be released on house arrest with a charge of that magnitude. I didn't belong there; all the miraculous signs were present for me to know that God will never leave me, nor forsake me, just like he promised in Deuteronomy 31:6.

CHAPTER 11
HOMEWARD BOUND

I walked out of Turner Gilford, escorted by a probation officer, and was taken back home. My wife and kids greeted me with so much love, and I could tell by the length of their hugs that they were feeling my pain and grateful to have me home.

Laura had prepared a hot meal for me, as she knew I was famished! The aroma of the food made my mouth salivate, but I couldn't partake just yet because the officer had to program my ankle bracelet.

After several attempts to activate the bracelet, he determined that the device was faulty. Wouldn't you know it? I was back in his car and being taken to another facility to get a monitor that worked. I was so outdone by this point as I felt like there was some type of bad luck looming over me. Once again, I kept repeating, "I will overcome this tribulation," as I was back in handcuffs and reliving the horrible experience again.

It was another hour of dealing with law enforcement before I was back at home to try this ankle monitor bullshit again. He discussed all the rules with me, and since the ankle bracelet was working, his job was complete, and I could be left alone with my family.

Laura filled me in on every detail of what happened since we separated. I was so curious to learn more about how she obtained my lawyer, which I might add is the only reason I was home. It's just a general fact that most black males are convicted because they didn't have the money to obtain a lawyer. She told me that she contacted a family member to inform them of the ordeal that took place and was given the name of "The Beast." She had never heard of him before, but as she continued to do her research, she learned that not only was he a former Prosecutor, but he had made several TV appearances and had built a great reputation for himself as a defense attorney. Laura was speaking so fast and left not one detail out. She said she called down to the police station and the jail several times, but couldn't get any information. She also called a bail bondsman to get me out, but even the bondsman said, "Mrs. Georges, there is no bond for this charge."

She was getting so emotional as she recapped what happened, and it was very emotional to see her this way. I tried to keep it together in front of the kids, but I knew I would unravel as soon as I got a moment to myself.

She continued to tell me that when The Beast went to the bond hearing, he had requested the police report, and the police station wouldn't release it. He had to get as much information from Laura instead of going in blind! She felt like they were drawing things out and ignoring our right to have the information. I knew exactly what she meant because I had already decided that I would report to the Bureau what happened and include this point she was making as well.

Laura just kept thanking God that I was home and kissing her teeth like Jamaicans do when they can't believe what's happening. She proceeded to tell me that she had to text photos of me to the lawyer so he could identify me in the courtroom. She was thankful that The Beast was understanding and determined to be there for me from the jump. He didn't allow obstacles to stand in his way because of COVID-19. He was our hero in the time of need.

My wife was busying herself in the kitchen. I knew that cooking for Mon Cheri was a form of therapy. I just watched her. And still, after all these years, I admire her resilience. It was a bit harder for me to look at my children because I never wanted them to see me entangled in the system or, even worse, involved in a murder case; this was around the time I was supposed to be going on college tours with my son Chris, and I was in my third week taking courses online to receive my master's in education.

I decided to slip away from everyone to take a shower because I could feel the overwhelm coming on. I let the shower run as I removed my clothes. I tried to get my pants from around my ankle monitor, and a wave of anger consumed me. I hated this so much. I silently screamed "why me, why me!" while fighting and swinging at the air.

Steam started filling the bathroom, and I stepped into the shower to rinse the filth off my body from the past 36 hours and the tears that were falling from my eyes. I washed my face over and over again and imagined that all of this was just a bad dream. It was all too real as I felt the soreness of my body from hitting the barrier.

After thirty minutes in the hot shower, the bathroom mirrors were covered in sweat, so I took my towel and wiped it away to examine myself. I wanted to make sure that when I left the bathroom, my family would see me as the loving father and husband I was, not the murderer they labeled me. But one thing is certain, and two things for sure: I was a changed man.

CHAPTER 12
HERE WE GO

It takes time to get used to a foreign object attached to your body. I tossed throughout the night, unconsciously shaking my leg to get that irritating ankle monitor off me. I couldn't rest soundly because I was wrestling with thoughts about the accident, thoughts about my future. With the little mental strength I had left, I found the power to think positively. At least I was at home, in my own bed, next to Laura, and not at TGK. I let out a deep sigh of relief and meditated on that till the next morning.

"The sun must be rising." I thought to myself. I heard Rambo shuffling in his cage. I got out of bed and stretched to get rid of some of the stiffness in my body. I slid on my house shoes and walked past the kitchen to the family room where Rambo sleeps. He wagged his tail so fast that I knew he was happy to see me. It's true what they say about dogs being a man's best friend. Rambo was white a medium-sized Coton breed. He had a strong bond with the family, and it was because of his loyalty that my family was safe. I doted on him even more while letting him jump on me so I could play rough with him. Before I let him out the sliding glass door, I moved the blinds back like a spy to see if the coast was clear. It's kinda messed up that going forward, what would usually be a simple task was feeling more like an episode out of The Walking Dead, where you know there's danger waiting for you somewhere out there. I guess this was my new way of thinking: that someone was out to get me.

I stepped outside with Rambo and took deep breaths to fill my lungs with fresh air. I watched him run about the yard along the side of the house towards our front gate. I knew exactly what he was doing. He was marking his territory and sniffing around. I took a seat on the patio chair and looked out at the nature preserve that was just beyond our fence. It was a designated area protected from humans to preserve the environment so plants and animals could thrive in their natural habitat. But what about me? Wasn't I created to provide my family with a safe and loving habitat? Don't I have the right to protect my family from danger, especially when it presents itself at your own front door? I began to go into deep thought, trying to make sense of my present situation. But the Bible tells us not to lean on our understanding. I had to keep living and watch what God can do.

I was a prisoner in my own home. Free but not free. And

not because of the federal mandate to shelter in place, but because of my legal status. I was being charged with murder. There goes that "M" word again.

I was only permitted to leave my home to go to church or the grocery store. I was already laid off and trying to get unemployment to help alleviate financial stress. Added to that were the hefty lawyer fees we had to pay monthly. It was like having a second mortgage. Laura and I started looking into all of our resources to be able to carry this burden.

As the day progressed, I settled into my usual spot on the sofa in the family room. Laura sat beside me and put her feet on the sofa to relax while we watched the evening news. Laura's ringtone sounded, and she checked her caller ID; it was my son's girlfriend calling. I could tell from her responses that the conversation was about me. Moments later, my phone goes off, and it's my homeboy Waiguy calling. I figured that news was spreading, and before I answered the call, I shook my head and said, "Here we go."

I answered the phone and said, "Hello." I could hear the confusion in his voice. He said, "Ellis, what's going on, man?" "Is what I'm seeing on the news true?" "They say you locked up". I said, "Listen, I'm home, man, the news ain't reporting it right." Meanwhile, I heard Laura repeating the same thing on her line. Waiguy was shocked and quite naturally curious to know what the real deal was. I told him I couldn't talk much about it because it was an open case and that what they said on the news was so far from the truth.

I remember seeing the news van on my street the day that it happened, but Laura made sure to have the officers keep them back. Plus, she wasn't interested in giving them a statement anyway. I assured Waiguy that I was okay and that I was just trying to keep my head up and to please pray for me during this difficult time.

He agreed, and then there was silence interrupted by a beep to notify me that another call was coming. I checked the caller ID, and it was my brother Johnny. I told Waiguy I appreciated the phone call, but I had to take another call.

I inhaled and let out a sigh to get ready for all the questions that would come my way. Johnny and I were very close, so I knew that he would be able to read between the lines without me having to explain all the details. I answered the phone and said, "Bro." And he said, "Yo, Bro, I can't believe this, I'm watching the news, and I'm tripping out." I said, "Brother, all we can do is pray and keep our faith in God and my attorney." I told him I couldn't talk long, and loved him and the family.

After I hung up the phone, I determined that that was the last call I would be taking for the night. I powered off my device and felt like throwing it at the TV. The news was saying all kinds of foolery and lies. I needed to call a family meeting to prepare Britt and Chris for what could potentially be the rockiest time of their lives.

I gathered everyone into the living room, and with a straight face, I told my family that things were about to get ugly. I knew that some of their friends would start calling, asking about what they saw on the news, so I advised them not to talk about it. Instead, just thank them for their concerns and be brief. I even encouraged them to stay strong and not to worry because everything would be fine. At least I prayed it would be, but God knows I was scared. A strange feeling took over me as I waited for my kid's reaction. It was the first time I needed them to support and hold me down. They both came over to me to offer their love and reassurance and said they would do as I asked.

I couldn't stop blaming myself for what happened. "Look what I'm putting my family through." I thought to myself. It was time for me to call it a night. I had no more energy left to endure another call that would come in on Laura's phone or to see a repeat headline of fake news.

I checked all the doors to my property with a heightened awareness for our safety. Once you've been robbed once or twice, you can never let your guard down. I retreated to my bedroom and vowed never to watch the news again. Besides, if I wanted to leave the house to clear my mind, that was impossible. I was under house arrest.

CHAPTER 13
CHANGED MAN

I was no longer the same man. I was a victim being victimized, and this shit was so unfair. Why did the "Bad Guy" have to come back to prey on us? This question would never be answered, no matter how much I tried to come up with a reason for his return. I needed badly to plead my case and advocate for myself. I had to get the truth out there to let people know that I was the victim and not a murderer. My head was thumping so hard that the pressure building up in my brain could explode at any minute. The series of events had me paranoid, and getting a sound night's sleep was impossible. I was having nightmares, and I just wanted to anesthetize the pain and drift off into complete darkness to keep from having visions of that dreadful day.

I was haunted by the faces of Robocop and the "Bad

Guy", and I would wake up from my sleep in cold sweats. I suffered from sleep deprivation, anxiety, depression, rejection, pity, and shame. I lost 12 pounds as a direct result of mental suffering that was now affecting my physical appearance. I was still without income and denied any compensation from unemployment or the additional stimulus money from the government. Unemployment stated that because I was arrested, I was automatically ineligible. Laura's income wasn't enough to cover all the monthly household expenses, plus the added lawyer fees. My back was against the wall, and as far as I'm concerned, I might as well have been pushed right through it. Being confined to my home and unable to work, I busied myself with my online schoolwork so I could feel like my life still had purpose.

Just days before all of this happened, I registered for an Organizational Communication for Adults Education & Training class at the University of Phoenix. I'd already had my Bachelor's degree, and it was my life's goal to obtain my Master's degree. My professor was no joke. She was brutally honest when critiquing my assignments, and her syllabus was packed with deadlines. She even rejected some of my assignments because they didn't meet her standards. I wanted to give her the excuse that I was in the midst of a crisis in hopes of her showing me some mercy. But I had no plans to share it with her. The number of times I entertained the thought of dropping out was like being on a seesaw. One minute, I was determined more than ever to finish; the next day was the complete polar opposite. I was ready to throw in the towel and say, "fuck it."

I needed to balance my emotions by finding that inner strength you never knew you had until the worst happened to you. My mind drifted back to the reasons my parents, especially my father, who left everything behind in Haiti (including me), to settle in America so I could one day receive a degree from an American institution. I chuckled to myself, as I could remember his lectures sounding the same every time, with his closing remarks being, "Remember, Ellis, if you want to make it in life, you need to be smart. So, make sure you study your books." I figured that with all my freedoms stripped away from me, knowledge was the one thing nobody could rob me of. I ended up getting an "A" in the course and a personal message from my professor that read, "Keep up the good work!"

I was not the only one who changed. Laura was going through unbelievable amounts of stress. She was working so hard to take care of the household and to finance my freedom. It was something I could not bear to watch. Since the mandate to shelter was in place, I finally understood how much she was responsible for at work. She managed projects that had her tied to her desk for hours. At times, I was afraid to look at her or even be near her because she would not respond to me the same way. She started becoming numb and, at times, wanted to isolate herself. I felt responsible for it all. I couldn't blame her, though, as she was the only one answering questions from The Beast and dealing with the case. She had to relive every detail countless times during the discovery calls, while all the while, I chose to evade it all for fear of a complete psychological breakdown.

Laura was just simply stronger than me in that respect. She was headstrong. Her mind operated like a GPS and could navigate and reroute if necessary to get to a destination. But how much more could she take on? Laura wore glasses, and I remember seeing her at her desk taking them off to rub her eyes and massage her temples to ease the tension. I told Laura to take a break from work, and that's when she unleashed all the pinned-up emotions she was suppressing. She threw her hands up and said, "Are you serious right now?" "Take a break?" "There is no time for that!" She ran down a laundry list of things she had to do, checked her watch, and told me exactly what time she had to finish it by. She continued to say, "I could have taken the promotion with another department to make more money," but I couldn't because I need the flexibility to work from home to be here for you. I feel like I'm doing it all by myself." Essentially, taking a break was out of the question for Laura.

I turned to walk away, feeling like shit; this was all my fault. I could see Chris peeking his head from the next room to see what was going on. Honestly, we were all affected and struggling internally to carry on with life as normal.

It was time to rinse the shame off my body and the tears welling up in my eyes down the shower drain again. It was only two in the afternoon, and my second shower of the day. Taking frequent showers became a coping mechanism and the only safe place where feeling completely broken as a man was allowed.

"God, why is this happening to me?" I said to myself. How could anyone be more stressed than me? I was the one facing life in prison with no parole, for Christ's sake. If things didn't work out in my favor, I would die in jail.

Once again, I was at my lowest point. When I needed a move from God, I chanted, "I will overcome this tribulation," over and over again.

Later that evening, Laura felt like talking, and I did as well. I was waiting for her cue to begin. She said she hated how things went earlier and that she recognized the Devil was trying to tear the family apart. I couldn't agree more with her, and I felt better already hearing her say that. Instantly, I could feel the connection between us again. She advised me that if I wanted a fighting chance of beating the case, we were going to need monetary help from our family and friends. She wanted to start a "GoFundMe" account because that's how desperate we were for the money. Chris even took a part-time job delivering pizza to make up for some of the financial lack, while my daughter, Brittney, stepped down from her job as an officer; she lost trust in the system because of how cruelly the officers treated me.

Who would have known that a month later, on May 25, 2020, the world would witness the murder of George Floyd by a white police officer in Minneapolis, Minnesota? The virus of police brutality against Blacks in America continues to spread like a plague.

For nine minutes and twenty-nine seconds, David Chauvin pressed his knee into Floyd's neck and back, cutting off his oxygen and killing him. He was mistreated by the officer and his peers, who, from the beginning, already found him guilty and sentenced him to death. He never had his day in court; instead, a racist officer who had no regard for a Black life found it convenient to take Floyd's life over a store clerk accusing him of using a counterfeit twenty-dollar bill. My God! It was a somber day in our household. The similarities with what happened to George prior to him taking his last breath, especially his last words, "I can't breathe," were like saying goodbye to a fallen soldier on the battlefield. That very well could have been me.

CHAPTER 14

BODY CAM

People all around the world marched and protested in solidarity against police brutality for weeks. I couldn't represent Mr. Floyd the way I would have wanted to because, of course, I was on lockdown. I wondered what the citizens in Miami thought of me when my case aired on the news or when they received the newspaper Monday morning at their front door. It's sad to say that I knew they would believe the lies the news told about me just because I was black.

Everything wasn't always about race for me, but after the accident, my lens was zoomed in, laser-focused on how the systemic challenges faced by Black people in America still exist. I truly believe that if the shoe were on the other foot and the "Bad Guy" was the homeowner and I was the robber, there would not be a case to argue.

Although my case wasn't as high profile as Floyd's, there was one journalist, however, who caught onto it. His name was C. Edwards. He compared my story to that of 3 white men, Gregory and Travis McMichael, along with William Bryan, who, in February of 2020, assumed Aubrey was a burglar and pursued him in their vehicle, ARMED, I remind you. They claimed they were trying to make a citizen's arrest, which resulted in a scuffle that led to the horrific death of Ahmaud Arbery.

Not one of them was arrested that day, as the responding officers treated them on a first-name basis. The D.A. told them specifically not to make any arrests. They sat comfortably in their homes, free to go as they pleased, until the video footage was released.

Edwards clearly painted the picture to his listeners that you have certain privileges in this country when you're White. One of them is the relationship that Whites have with law enforcement. It was like some unspoken contract between them, having favorable terms that Blacks didn't get. For centuries, this has been the plight of a Black man. This virus of hate and white supremacy is still breathing across America. It would cost me everything to fight for my freedom, and I mean that literally. No matter the cost, I was prepared to do anything to prove my innocence. God saw fit to spare my life that weekend. I still had breath in my body, unlike George, unlike Ahmaud, unlike the other Black men before me who were brutalized and murdered by the police.

Three months had passed, and it was finally the day to

meet my defense attorney in person. The Beast had been a hero to me, and because my future depended heavily on his expertise, I prayed for him nightly to win my case. I looked forward to the drive that day. It had been months since I was able to leave my home or allowed to drive. His office was in Broward County, about 30 minutes out. Laura talked a lot about the case and mentioned what she wanted to tell The Beast. I could remember looking out of the window and having a nostalgic moment of the day I took that taxi ride from the airport to Queen's house when I first arrived in the U.S.. How feelings of excitement and anticipation swirled about my body as I was thrilled to be living the American dream. That was a pivotal moment in my life. However, that joyful memory was blotted out by the GPS, alerting us that we were arriving at our destination, bringing me back to reality. To be honest, I was slowly dying inside as, with each passing day, the American Dream was turning into the American Nightmare.

Laura parked the car, and we both got out, fixing our clothes and checking ourselves for any imperfections. That's one thing Laura and I had in common: we both knew how to clean up nicely.

I was impressed by how beautiful The Beast's office was. Upon entry, I noticed the vibrant purple paint on the walls and a huge purple crystal on display. It was a spacious office with a window facing a lake. Normally, I wouldn't be so wowed by the scenery, but with my freedom on the line, I began filling my memory bank with images of the beautiful view just in case the worst happened, and prison doors and brick walls would be the everyday scenery.

I finally got to shake hands with The Beast and meet him face to face. I expected him to be dressed up in a designer suit with shiny black leather shoes and wearing a Rolex watch. Boy, was I wrong! When I saw him step into the office wearing a white tee and a pair of blue jeans, I couldn't believe how casual he was. He put me in the mind frame of Tony Danza from the sitcom, "Who's The Boss."

I felt totally at ease when I finally got to shake hands with my lawyer. Meanwhile, he and Laura had already established a relationship and carried on like good friends. Once we got past the formalities, I opened up to him and told him that every day since the accident, I had blamed myself for what happened, and the pressure of it all was taking a toll on me. He looked at me and said, "Ellis, you can only blame yourself one time, and one time only." He spoke in a manner like a father coaching his son through a rough patch, and his words resonated deeply with me. He gave Laura and me a book that he wrote in hopes that my mindset would change for the better. I guess from his experience, he has seen clients display all kinds of emotional distress and felt compelled to write a self-help book.

We began to discuss the facts of the case. It was never easy for me to relive the events of those two days, but I answered every question in complete detail so The Beast can do what he does best. Plus, it was my life that was on the line, and I wanted to be involved in every aspect of obtaining my freedom. I told The Beast about the harsh treatment the officers put me through, and I requested the body cam footage to help support my claim when I went to the Bureau.

I expressed to my lawyer that I couldn't believe I was being charged with 2nd-degree murder. Just saying those words sent chills through my body, and instantly, that horrid feeling returned. The Beast responded with these words, "I will see to it that you won't spend a day in jail, Ellis."

I left his office with more hope than I walked in with. I am not going to lie; that was the reassurance I needed to make it through this nightmare. I got some good sleep that night.

CHAPTER 15
OH THE LIES

"This guy has a rifle fully loaded!" "He killed him!" the officer said. Turn off your camera!" he yelled to his comrade. I couldn't believe what I was hearing as I watched the body cam footage. There was speculation from the jump that I had killed a man before the investigation began. This false information trickled down, and I was appalled and instantly sickened at the incorrect assumption from the officer.

But it doesn't stop there. I would be remiss if I didn't talk about the photos of my car right after the accident and the photos of my car after the investigation. The photos showed a clear distinction that there was some foul play going on. My car's battery wire and engine belt had been cut, and the front end of my vehicle was even more damaged than I remembered. This corrupt behavior displayed by the detectives was sure to strip me of my family. On the other hand, there was absolutely no report of the "Bad Guy's" criminal past; it was just speculation about me, and it's all on tape.

What in the "Blue Fuck" was going on with the criminal justice system, I thought to myself. If you don't agree that law enforcement treats Blacks differently than Whites, then why wasn't Kyle Rittenhouse arrested on August 25, 2020, after killing two people at a Black Lives Matter protest?

He crossed state lines with a Smith & Wesson MP5 rifle, and the police did not do anything! He was given water and was allowed to return to his home without being charged. After going to trial, he was acquitted of the charges because his lawyer argued that it was self-defense.

According to the experts, approximately 2,067 inmates are on death row, with 40% being African American. The highest arrest rates were for people of color and minority defendants, who received harsher punishments for similar crimes than their White counterparts. Do you want to talk about the odds being stacked against me? My God, how could I be in this predicament? After going through the initial arrest and now having to wait for the outcome of my case, I felt like I was being buried alive. The sad reality is that my life depended on the facts. And the facts were already tainted by a corrupt system.

I fulfilled a promise to myself and filed a complaint at the Professional Compliance Bureau. I needed to tell them how horribly Robocop and Frankenstein treated me, and I wanted them to feel the repercussions. This device on my foot tracked my every move, so I had to get permission from my probation officer to go down there.

I was confident that all three hours of the body cam evidence would be enough for them to take disciplinary actions. When I arrived at the Bureau, I spoke briefly with two Sergeants and explained my situation. They took the footage to their Superior Officer, who would review what was on it. I was prepared to wait as long as it took, but within fifteen minutes, the two Sergeants came back and reported that after reviewing the evidence, there was no probable cause to open an internal affairs investigation.

I had to pause for a moment to think of the right response to that statement. I told the officers that it was hard for me to believe that within 15 minutes, they were able to determine that nothing they saw on the footage was cause for concern, especially since it was over three hours long. In a dry tone, one of the officers said, "Well, we fast-forwarded the video."

I looked at both and said, "Really," using a type of tone to insinuate that I knew someone was bull-shitting me. One officer said, "If you want, we can still make a report and talk to the arresting officer, but we did not see that he left you in the car without AC for hours. I had to reiterate the same question about whether they watched the entire video just to be sure I got this right. They gave the same response of "Yes." I knew that my time there was over and that there was absolutely no need to carry on. I thanked both officers for their time and left the Compliance Bureau wondering if I were a White man, would things play out the same way?

This experience had retrained my thinking about law enforcement and the criminal justice system. I had every right to believe that because of the color of my skin, I was dealing with racist cops, while on the other hand, I was smart enough to know that not all those who put on the badge and uniform were crooked and wanted to protect innocent civilians from the bad guys.

The echoing sound of "I will overcome this situation" stirred up in my gut as I was figuring out a way to go over their heads because Miami Dade Police didn't serve or protect me that day.

I reached out to some of our local community leaders and our congressman in office to address the incident. I was unable to speak with the congressman on the first try. However, he called me back, and we talked for a few minutes. Ultimately, he wanted me to complete a privacy release form, and then he would get back to me. But nothing came of it.

Are we, as Black and Minority people, only taken seriously when we show up in massive numbers to be heard? Are the politicians only ranting about ensuring "equal rights" for minorities to get our votes, so they can just get in office and then disregard the injustices happening every day to minority individuals? This experience I was going through continued to suck the life out of me. I was trying to do everything right, and nothing or no one who was in a direct position to help did anything. Martin Luther King and Malcolm X were fighting for equality using two different approaches, and I clearly see why.

Again, I had to find balance and shake off any ill thoughts that were filtering through my head. My cell phone started ringing, and I didn't even feel like talking. After the incident, I was dodging a lot of calls, but this call was one I had to take. I looked at my caller ID, and it was my bonus mother-in-law, Pamela, calling. She was so special to Laura and me, even more so because Queen was gone. It must have been divine intervention because I was about to lose my cool. Her spiritual and mental support had such a positive effect on me that I chose to remain positive and let the Almighty see me through. God kept showing me that he was sending the right people at the right time to comfort me through this ordeal. He did that by sending "The Beast" to represent me.

CHAPTER 16
ANGER ISSUES

It was early September 2020 when there was a breakthrough in the case, and a plea deal was on the table. The Beast went back and forth with the Prosecutor, a White woman who was already so disgusted that I wasn't behind bars waiting for sentencing. It was her job to defend the deceased and represent the family who wanted to see me in prison, and she was fierce about it. He continued to say that after the negotiations, the Prosecutor was willing to reduce the 2nd-degree murder charge to Vehicular Homicide, and also charged me with leaving the scene of the accident. The deal would come with 4 ½ years of jail time.

Arrogance and anger overtook me, and before I knew it, I told The Beast, "You could do more than that!" I wanted him to understand that I didn't want to admit that I was responsible for his death. It was the "Bad Guy's" actions and choices that caused his demise. Laura was appalled at my outburst and said, "Yo ass could be behind bars right now." "You need to calm down!"

I was angry, and looking back on things, I realized I had the right to be. I felt it in my gut that a better deal could be afforded to me. I felt confident that if we went to trial, the jury would find me credible and would have no other option than to render a decision of not guilty. The Beast disagreed with my thinking and said that we could go to trial if I wanted to, but he made it abundantly clear that going to trial would increase my chances of incarceration.

I held off on deciding and requested my lawyer to continue negotiating. Within weeks, a second plea bargain was on the table, which was two years of community control, eight years of probation, 200 hours of community service, and my license being suspended for life. He expressed that taking the proposed plea deal would be in my favor, and as he assured me, I wouldn't have to spend a day behind bars. I know this should have been a no-brainer, but making this decision was complex.

Clearing my name meant more to me than anything. He also reminded me that leaving my fate to a jury would result in a harsher sentence, so I needed to consider all these factors. Also, with that, the amount of time and money it would cost me to fight for my innocence was something I just couldn't afford. This predicament I was in made it obvious why most Black men are incarcerated. Without a substantial amount of money, one facing jail time usually takes a plea bargain. I have fallen into that category.

I needed time to think things through and talk about what I was feeling to someone I could vent to. One of my buddies who stayed in contact with me gave me some of the best advice that had the ability to help me see straight. He said, "Ellis, listen to your lawyer." "You don't want to take any chances by going to trial and throwing your life away for a guy like that." He said, "They can assassinate your character, but they cannot kill your spirit." That was another divine moment because immediately I felt God's presence and the sound of the Queen's voice saying, "God did not promise us a life without trials, that in order for good to happen, we have to experience the worst."

I just wanted 2020 to be over, in all honesty. I wished for this nightmare to end so I could try to move forward with my life. After much prayer and consideration, I was ready to take the plea deal. I couldn't live with the suspense of not knowing my fate anymore. It was taking a toll on my health, mentally and physically.

One night in the winter, I was having trouble sleeping again. I stayed up until 3 a.m., just looking up at the ceiling in my bedroom while shifting that God-awful ankle monitor that was making me so uncomfortable. The house was completely quiet except for the light snoring Laura had going on next to me. It was out of the blue when I saw a flash of lightning followed by thunder.

It wasn't a loud clapping sound of thunder but more of a

rolling sound that had a soothing effect on me. I began to think deeply about the fact that I could make the best out of my situation, continue to go to school, and use my life experience to mentor someone. I could feel a smile spread across my face because I had found myself again, and it felt good. I connected with a part of me that had been replaced with self-sabotage, shame, and believing the worst about myself.

I drifted off to sleep, and the dream I had was one that I would never forget. In my dream, I heard a lot of people cheering and chanting, and I saw something like a celebration in the streets of Haiti. I was my younger self, like 12 years old or so. I was pushing through the crowd so I could see what all the excitement was about. In the middle of all those people was my grandmother dancing and shouting "Mesi Bondye," which means "Thank you, God" in Creole. It was like the people were praising God for another victory. Yaya reached her hands out for me to dance with her, and all the people around me, with huge smiles on their faces, cheered me on!

The impact of that dream woke me right out of my sleep, and that marked the beginning of my acceptance of what happened on April 25th, 2020.

The Spirit fell on me so hard that I had to get out the bed and head to the shower again. I released so many emotions in the shower and thanked God for his comfort and breakthrough I received. I've heard countless testimonies from others who said God came through for them in the midnight hour. I held onto the glorious revelation I received from the dream. I didn't have to be ashamed anymore that God still loves me, and my family didn't crucify me; they supported me.

I turned off the shower and began to study myself in the mirror. I looked at my broad nose and lips and turned my face side to side, examining my dark skin. How could my appearance make someone discriminate against me? Their preconceived notions of me being a criminal were all because I was a Black Man. But I had to shake off all the stigmas that leach themselves to Black people in this country, the stereotypes of violence, the economic disparities, mental health stigmas, negative portrayals in the news, and so on and so forth. I had to start seeing myself the way God sees me. I knew by the power behind my dream that God had forgiven me for my actions that day, and he released me from the grief I caused the family of the deceased, as well as the strain I put my own family under. I made the decision to take the plea deal.

CHAPTER 17
IT'S A CELEBRATION

2021 was a defining year for my loved ones. My wife's cousin was sending invitations for her 50th birthday party in April, and my son Chris was soon to graduate from high school. As for myself, I was on course to graduate with my Master's Degree in Education in the fall. Positive things were on the horizon, and, based on my lawyer's prediction, the case was moving fast, and the court proceedings would begin soon. A family getaway would be just the relief I needed before it was time to face the music of reliving that dreadful day in court.

I could feel Laura beginning to relax and breathe a little easier since I took the plea bargain. I could hear the excitement in her voice as she told family members about her baby Chris's upcoming graduation. She wanted it to be very special and hoped the mandates would be lifted so the family could attend like normal.

A trip to Tampa would be perfect timing for me, and especially my wife, to decompress from all the madness. Laura loved her family, and anytime she got a chance to be around her mother, aunts, uncles, and cousins meant the world to her. Everybody loved Laura. It was just that simple. Despite the tons of pressure she was under, Laura was just that family member you could depend on to be there for you no matter what. She could have declined the invitation and come up with some really good excuses as to why she couldn't attend, but her circumstances didn't trump her belief in "family over everything."

I just hated that I couldn't move about freely like I wanted to. In my opinion, being on house arrest was far better than being in jail, but both were mentally tormenting. I needed this trip, along with a change of scenery, to uplift my mind and escape being confined to my home.

Appearing in court and wearing that annoying ankle monitor was not on my favorite thing to-do list. I had to request permission from the Judge to travel as part of the court orders. As a grown man, this wasn't the flex I imagined for myself. It was belittling in a sense, making me feel like a little boy who needed permission from his mom to go somewhere. Thankfully, the request was granted by the Judge, and just like that little boy would react when his mom said yes to his request, I grabbed a fist full of air and pulled down with all my might, and without screaming, I muffled a "Yes!" trying to contain my excitement!

Ocean air and the white sands of Clearwater, Florida, were the scenery for the next three days. All the family started to arrive at the Airbnb and nearby hotels along the beach, and before you knew it, the sounds of reggae music and the smell of garlic, onion, thyme, and jerk seasoning filled the air. Laura and her cousin Marcia, the birthday girl, were top chefs, and so were her Mother, Pamela, and Auntie Sue. They had already planned out their menu for three days and placed me on grill duty. West Indians didn't play about their food or music. Add good company and a game of dominoes to the equation; equaled a damn good time!

The backyard of the Airbnb was simply fitting for the occasion. It had a nice-sized pool and a tiki hut that was perfect for entertainment! The vibes felt amazing, and just the interaction with family sure felt better than FaceTime or Zoom meet-ups! The birthday girl had planned an extravagant weekend to celebrate her 50th birthday. The welcome barbecue was a success, followed by a beach day where all the family wore matching T-shirts in honor of Marcia! It was so cool watching my little cousins play along the shore, running back and forth, showing off the seashells they'd collected, while the "over the hill" crew sat under a tent drinking Heinekens and chatting about the old days.

Laura didn't pay me much attention at all, and I wasn't even upset about it. She was bonding with the women in her family, and I knew she needed their love and affection badly.

I missed seeing her laugh uncontrollably until her stomach hurt! Her cousin Marcia laughed even harder than Laura did, and it was so contagious that I had to crack a smile and chuckle myself just watching them two. Lately, I'd gotten used to making myself invisible most of the day. I forgot what it felt like to let loose and be free. This was the vibe I wanted for my son's graduation day, just some good ole family, food & fun.

It was our last night in Tampa, and the Star Ship Yacht was the venue for our formal night to close out the birthday weekend. A two-hour dinner cruise sailing on the waters of Tampa Bay, watching the sunset, was magical. The yacht was simply beautiful, docked along the pier and waiting for the guests to board. Everyone was dressed up, looking lovely in their attire, and my wife and I couldn't remember the last time we had a romantic evening out. Everyone had their cell phones out, snapping photos to memorialize the occasion.

Dinner on the yacht with a live DJ and a special toast to the birthday girl was the bomb! While everyone was chatting with each other after dinner, it was the perfect opportunity for me to go up to the open deck to take in the view of downtown Tampa. The cool ocean air felt good on my skin, and inhaling the scent of the salt water instantly made me think of Haiti.

The reality of my life would just hit me, and my mind would start to drift off into the abyss where no positive thoughts existed. "What time was it?" I thought to myself. It's been a pattern of mine that just about 7 pm every night, I thought of him and the events that took place both days at my home. Britt and Chris stayed behind, and I felt uneasy about not being there for the past few days. But I had faith in my little buddy Rambo to be on guard in my absence to alert the kids if he sensed danger. According to the charges brought up against me, I killed a man using my vehicle. No matter how hard I tried to block out this traumatic experience, it haunted me every day, sending chills up my spine and elevating my heart rate with the same intensity as when it all unfolded.

I don't know what's harder to endure: my parents traveling 700 miles on a tiny sailboat drifting away from their homeland, risking their lives in search of a better future, or me standing on a 180 ft luxury yacht suffering from PTSD, privately having a meltdown. It didn't really matter one way or another. We all made a decision, hoping for the best outcome, and whatever came along with it, we just have to endure.

CHAPTER 18

POMP AND CIRCUMSTANCE

O nly two family members were able to attend Chris' graduation, and as a proud father and super proud big sis, Britt and I were preparing to leave for the big event. Laura insisted we go while she stayed back to set up for the small gathering we were having at our home. She hired an amazing Chef to prepare a special meal and ordered specialty desserts and cookies with the Class of '21 written on them. Streaming the ceremony was an option, and I know Laura was only pretending when I asked her if she was sure that she wanted to stay. She said in a convincing tone, "Noooo, Ellis, it's ok." "I can watch it online." It's something about when the baby of the family graduates. As a parent, you feel like you did your job of supporting your kids through the public school system from kindergarten to twelfth grade, and now you can woosah.

Ensuring your child's success in school meant attending parent-teacher conferences, helping with homework, and the constant ripping and running that comes with the extracurricular activities your child participated in. I gave Laura all the credit for making Chris and Britt's school days successful.

I kissed her goodbye and headed out with the graduate. As I reached in for a kiss, I couldn't help but notice how gray Laura's hair was getting. She wasn't seeing her stylist like normal, and I instantly interpreted it as me being the reason why my wife was graying so rapidly. She was carrying my burdens and trying to be my savior. I hurried out of the house, shaking my head in sync with the internal humming of um, um, um because I was disappointed with myself.

On the car ride to the ceremony, I contemplated having a serious talk with Chris about the importance of making good decisions in life now that he was an adult. I didn't want to ruin the moment by projecting my negative experience on him, but I feared for my son's life in a way I'd never felt before. Chris was a mellow kid with a good head on his shoulders. He didn't leave the house much and never gave his mom or me any reason not to trust his actions or decisions. He had already stepped up as a man and decided to enroll in a local college and take on a full-time job instead of going away to school because of my circumstances, so I decided to drop the talk for now and chill.

Before the ceremony began, I glanced around, looking at everyone seated in the auditorium with their face mask on, practicing social distancing. The virus was all anyone spoke about then. "Do you have your mask?" "Are you going to get the vaccine?" "You think the government is experimenting on us?" Around this time, the vaccine was made available to all ages 16 and older. While sitting there, I thought, "What could the keynote speaker say to encourage the graduates in the face of uncertainty?" I myself was having a hard time coming up with the right words to encourage my son about his future.

"Pomp and Circumstance" began playing; everyone knew what that meant. The Class of 2021 entered the room and started their march down the aisle, and the ceremony was underway. I snapped out of the thoughts swirling in my head, shifted my weight in my seat, and focused on what mattered most: Chris.

As a soon-to-be graduate myself, getting my master's in education really made me get into the moment even more. I knew the teachers were just as proud of those students they taught and connected with. That was truly the fuel and passion for me. Ellis "Education" Georges may have well been my middle name. I enjoyed being in an environment filled with education and enriching the minds of the youth who would later become the future of this country. This graduation ceremony meant so much more to me, not just because Chris was my son, but because of the 360 moment I was experiencing. It was awakening. It was like a cartoon flip book where, one by one, all the frames from my past right up until that very moment formed a clear picture. My parents' chief reason for coming to America was for my schooling, and I knew if they were living, they would be so proud to know that now I see the benefit and beauty of possessing a certain level of knowledge. The enlightenment of one's mind is its benefit, and the fact that no one could take that knowledge away was its beauty.

Britt & I cheered as loud as we could when Chris' name was called! We jumped up and down and tried to get the best photos of his moment in time! I learned to take nothing for granted as I reminded myself that I could have been behind bars, but because of God's goodness towards me, I was physically in the building. God knows I couldn't handle that guilt I would have felt if I missed it. I low-key wondered if Laura was really ok. While I cheered for Chris, I simultaneously was thinking about her.

On the ride back home, Britt and I told Chris how proud of him we were countless times. Chris' mannerisms were so laid back, but when he spoke, it was always so profound, and he never forgot to acknowledge God or leave you with something positive. That was the same for both of my kids, actually. Chris listened to us praise him for a job well done, and his response was simple. "God is good," he said each time. I told Chris that I was pleased that he was able to keep his head up and stay positive throughout this ordeal. He reiterated what the keynote speaker said, "We have to have faith and not fear if we are to endure this difficult time." In his own words, he added, "We can only go up from here, pops." It made me emotionally weak on the inside, and if I weren't a pro at holding back tears, I would have needed some Kleenex to blot them dry.

CONGRATULATIONS CHRIS! Everyone shouted as we entered our home from the ceremony. Suzy's cousin Marcia, who was also his godmother, was grinning from ear to ear, along with his aunt and uncle, who were visiting from Maryland, along with a few close friends. In the entryway of our home, we have what we call the "Wall of Fame." All our diplomas from high school to college were strategically placed on the wall with three designated spots to hang Chris's next, then mine, and then eventually Laura's. That's how much education meant to us, that even in our daily coming in and out of our homes, it served as a reminder of our great achievements. Opposite that wall were our wedding pictures and family portraits. If you were a guest visiting us, it would be very evident upon arrival that the Georges were about Faith, Family, and Education. Needless to say, the graduation party superseded my expectations as the feelings I got from the trip to Tampa overflowed into my home. Good vibes, great food, and company brought us so much happiness.

CHAPTER 19
I APOLOGIZE

F lorida was treacherously hot this time of year, as August's humidity levels, on average, were 66%, with a high chance of showers and thunderstorms daily. I opened the sliding glass door to let Rambo out after being in his kennel all night. I grabbed the remote control and turned on the TV to catch the weather report and to see what transpired overnight. Most South Floridians knew that hurricane season was nothing to play with. The news reporter said Hurricane Ida was making her way toward Louisiana and was projected to weaken significantly as it headed toward Miami. I, on the other hand, was dealing with my own personal storm as my final court date was just around the corner on September 17th. I was also preparing to attend my graduation ceremony, which was being held in Georgia at the World Congress Center the week after. Both events gave me anxiety in a way, but I was ready to put this all behind me.

Obviously, I needed permission to travel again, but the more pressing matter was that apology letter I had to write at the Prosecutor's request. I didn't feel like I needed to apologize for the accident, but because of my integrity and being raised by good parents who taught me that it's ok to say sorry even if you're not wrong, I had to do it. I could hear Queen saying, "You will find peace within yourself, and that is better than regret." It still amazes me how your mind can recall things that once sounded so silly and interpret them later on in life to be the most profound thing you've ever heard. That's the effect Queens' wisdom had on me, especially during my time of despair.

I went to the desk in the living room that Laura had turned into an office. I opened the laptop and opened a Word document. I had a notepad on the side of the laptop just in case I needed to scribble some thoughts down. I stared at the blank document with my fingers resting on the keyboard, just waiting for the words to come. I typed up a few words, then tapped the backspace button until I deleted it all. I did this a few times, then gently closed the laptop and rolled away from my desk. I rested my elbows on my knees and dropped my head in my hands to rub my temples as I tried to relieve the tension that was beginning to build.

Corrupt thoughts began to stir up as I felt as if somebody owed me a damn apology for ruining my entire life! And what about those cops who left me in the car that day to die from heat exhaustion? Where was my apology? I should call The Beast and have him demand an apology letter from the family, the officers, and everyone else involved who made my life a living hell. Trouble came looking for me that day. Not once, but twice! Why? Why? Why did this have to happen? I was so wrapped up in my feelings that it wasn't until I tasted the salty tears on my lips and noticed the teardrops that landed on the floor that I realized I was having a meltdown. I really wanted to begin writing, but I just couldn't find the right words. Then the peace that surpasses all understanding overtook me right when I started to unravel. The Holy Spirit reminded me of the crucifixion of the Savior. Jesus Christ, who was nailed to a cross while being ridiculed, laughed at, and sentenced to death, said, "Father, forgive them, for they know not what they do." Having compassion towards those who wrongfully persecute you was the answer for me to push through the pain and suffering. Compassion would allow me to get through my writer's block. I repeated my mantra, "I will overcome this tribulation." I simply had to persevere because there was much more to endure since I accepted the plea bargain. For example, hours of community service to do, my driver's license being revoked, and did I mention the new name that would be bestowed upon me after the Judge slams his gavel to conclude the case? "Felon!" Yeah, that's the part that stings the most. That classification would never be one I accept. And being my own judge and defense attorney, I object and will never honor that name because, in my opinion, justice isn't really justice after all.

I wiped the tears from my face with the white tee I was wearing and gripped the desk to pull myself forward to type the apology letter. I completed it in less than an hour, and like Queen said, I found peace within myself. I did what had to be done.

In the days leading up to my court date, I practiced in the mirror how I would present myself in the courtroom. I was testing out different facial expressions and body language, hoping the Judge would see me as an honest man who was just standing my ground and protecting my family. Nothing I saw in the mirror looked or felt natural, so I shrugged off the idea and decided I would just let it ride. I wondered if the listeners in the courtroom would understand me clearly when I spoke because my accent was still very strong. My biggest fear was reciting an apology that the family of the deceased would consider bullshit or couldn't comprehend. I was strong enough to handle the situation, either way the pendulum would swing. Ultimately, I belonged to God, who is the Author and Finisher of my life. It is His will that I would have to accept.

I spent time going through my closet, picking out the suits I would wear—one for the court date and one for the graduation. I opted for an olive-colored suit with a black shirt, black shoes, and an olive tie. I figured after I wore the suit, I knew I would never wear it again. It would just become an artifact, kind of like they do with celebrities' garments that you see at a museum with a caption below it. Mine would read, "Ellis Georges wore this suit before the Court on September 17, 2021, where he was convicted of vehicular homicide." I still couldn't believe it.

Laura and Chris would ask me more frequently how I was feeling, as they could only imagine what I must've been going through leading up to the court date. I knew this was just their way of supporting me, even though, at times, it made me uncomfortable. Once again, it was my actions that put us in this predicament in the first place, and I battled with self-forgiveness. Britt was really the one I worried about the most, as she seemed to be totally withdrawn from the situation. My baby girl had experienced the cruelties of society and prejudices firsthand through my experience, and it was turning her warm heart cold. With all that being said, the citizens of Florida dodged Hurricane Ida with minimal damage and went on with their lives as normal.

CHAPTER 20
TIME TO FACE THE MUSIC

Today was the day that the Judge would go over the details of my plea bargain and make sure I clearly understood the limitations that would be placed on my life. I woke up every hour the night before, anticipating this very moment. Having to face the family and that Prosecutor who was out to destroy me had me tossing and turning all night. Thank God I had my clothes already laid out. My wife wore a black blouse and a beautiful Tiffany blue suit. She wore a pearl choker around her neck, and if you were to see us strolling down the street, you would think we were some executives on our way to a business meeting of some sort. Honestly, I wish that was the case because who would have known that I was wearing an ankle monitor beneath my clothes? The County was watching my every move as they deemed me a flight risk. Anyway, my son Chris was dressed and ready to go, looking sharp in his button-down white shirt, slacks, and brown shoes. He was just like his mom and me. He knew how to dress appropriately for any occasion. Laura made sure we all had on that other accessory, which was our facemask, and I grabbed the folder that secured the apology letter.

I could remember pulling up to the courthouse and Laura saying to him so sternly, "Chris, I don't ever want to see you in this building unless you're a lawyer. Try your hardest to stay out of trouble." The site of a courthouse for a black person just never gave off any positive vibes. It was like a symbol of injustice and many unfair verdicts that were handed down to people of color over the centuries. Chris responded in his reserved manner with a "Yes, Ma'am." He and I both understood her exact reason for speaking this way. It was a lot for anyone to bear seeing their loved one being tangled up in the system. Not to mention the fact that fighting for justice was expensive as well.

As we entered the courtroom, I greeted my lawyer and gave him the apology letter. He handed it to the Prosecutor, and I could see her scan over it, then handed it back and told The Beast that it was unacceptable because it didn't state what I did that day. Didn't she know what I went through to get the apology letter done? After The Beast gave it back to me, I folded it up and passed it back to Laura, who was sitting right behind me.

"All rise!" The familiar command that the bailiff belted out had everyone on their feet. It was time for me to face the music and move forward with my life. Taking his rightful seat behind the wooden bench was The Honorable Judge J. I've seen him over a Zoom meeting before, but this was my first time seeing him in person. He was a White man who looked to be in his late fifties. He was wearing a black facemask that concealed the rest of his facial features, but by the sound of his voice, he seemed to be a very calm, collected individual who might have a pleasant appearance. He had me stand and raise my right hand to swear to tell the truth, and I did as he asked. I could feel my body getting hot as adrenaline and nervousness rushed through me. He began the hearing with a series of questions, and because of my nervousness, I bombed the first one he asked! He asked me if anyone forced or threatened me to accept the plea bargain, and I answered with a "Yes." The Beast jumped up so fast and asked the Judge to please repeat the question, as he believed his client (me) didn't understand. I was shaking in my boots, but I answered correctly the second time around. I started to listen more intently to each question asked to avoid messing up again. His line of questioning was over, and just like that, the Judge handed down my fate as I agreed to the plea deal.

I took my seat and watched as the mother of the "Bad Guy" got up to address the court. She spoke about how much she loved her son. In her exact words, she said, "The only son I had, and now he's gone," tore me up inside, as a parent. I understood her grief. The "Bad Guy's" father did not appear in court that day, but I believe that he tried to get through to his son by telling him the truth and the consequences behind his behavior, while his mother chose to only see her son as an angel. Either way, the situation was so complex, and no matter how you interpret it, so many people were affected by his actions that day.

Before the closing of the hearing, the Honorable Judge J asked if I had anything to say, and I said, "Yes, your Honor." It was time to man up and speak my peace, no matter what anyone thought of me, plus I had to do it for the fallen victims who never had an opportunity. The courtroom was completely silent as I looked back at Laura and motioned for her to pass me the apology letter that the Prosecutor turned down. With shaky hands, I unfolded the letter and stood to my feet. At that moment, I recalled that all of this was being streamed live on Zoom for all to watch. I knew I had family and friends tuning in, and that meant a lot. I started to inhale very deeply to calm my nerves, and I noticed that Laura stood up and lowered her head with her hands crossed in front of her in a posture of prayer and respect. It was confirmation that she had my back, and I knew she was praying for my strength to get through this.

I began to read the apology that God placed on my heart.

September 17, 2021

Dear Members of the Family,

Today, I want to express my sadness and the sorrow I have felt for the loss of your son. I can only imagine the pain that I have caused. On Saturday, April 25, 2020, my actions were not of malicious intent. It was to scare him and let him know he had been seen doing wrong and, hopefully, would not return to my home to cause my family any harm. I do not feel anyone deserves to perish this way. I prayed and asked God for forgiveness for my actions on April 25th, 2020

TODAY, I am expressing my most profound remorse and asking you to forgive me as well. You may not know me, but ask anyone who does, and they'll tell you I am not a violent person. I have never harmed anyone nor wished to cause harm or pain to anyone. The result of the incident on April 25th was not intentional. I ask respectfully for your forgiveness and understanding. THANK YOU.

I took my seat after that.

The air was so thick in the courtroom that you could have cut it with a knife. The Judge looked over some documents and broke the silence when he looked at the Prosecutor and said, "This man has no criminal record." He was saying it in a manner where he couldn't agree with the harshness of some of the charges. The Prosecutor knew this about me and still went for the jugular. The Beast informed him that I would graduate a week later with a master's degree. You could see the shock factor on his face, even with him wearing a mask! He looked at me and said "Is that right, Mr. Georges?" and I said, "Yes." He asked what my degree was, and I told him in Education. He was amazed that I was able to push forward and stay on course after everything that happened. The Honorable Judge dropped the charge of leaving the scene, and I was so thankful. He saw the good in me, and believe it or not, the Prosecutor was so moved during the reading of the letter that she wanted a copy of it. Something in the atmosphere shifted the hearts and minds of the people in that room. There was physical evidence of forgiveness that only a move of God can achieve.

We walked out of the courtroom, and The Beast and I hugged and shook hands with short bursts of intensity, as this was a win for both of us.

My wife wandered off in the direction of the Prosecutor, who had taken a seat on a bench. According to Laura, she was still very emotional about the case and wiped tears from her eyes. She admitted that she felt empathy for Ellis but had a job to do. Laura asked if she could approach the mother of the deceased and personally offer a word of peace on behalf of her family, and she agreed. Laura felt that was the Christian thing to do because we truly never meant for anyone to lose their life that day.

CHAPTER 21

MY LIFE, MY LIFE, MY LIFE

One night, in a dream, I walked with the Lord by the beach. There were two footprints, mine and the Lord's. But during tough times, I just saw mine, and I wondered why. So, I asked the Lord, "Why leave me alone when I was down?" The Lord said, "My precious child, I never left you during your times of suffering; when you saw only one set of footprints, it was then that I carried you." Author-Unknown.

I often wonder how a poem known around the world didn't have a person's name or identity attached to it. I would have loved to learn about the author's trials and tribulations that allowed him or her to pen such a magnificent piece of poetry that could be found in a picture frame hung in so many homes.

The author may have purposefully left out his or her name for the millions of believers who suffered trials to claim as their own testimony. I became enlightened by the fact that it wasn't necessary for me to go into details when asked, "How did I make it through?" I could respond by simply saying "Footprints in the Sand" to alleviate the pain I felt every time I had to relive this tribulation.

After returning home from the courthouse, my emotions vacillated from celebration to disappointment. It played out in my mind something like, "I'm not going to prison, yay," to "I'm a Felon with no job, suspended license, eight years' probation, two more years of house arrest, two hundred hours of community service.

I took note of Laura's demeanor as she drove back home, shaking her head and releasing sounds of hmm, hmm, hmm. I knew she was internalizing everything that had just taken place. When Laura couldn't find the words to express herself, it usually meant that she was praising and thanking God for another miracle he performed. She dropped her purse and came towards me. She whispered, "I told you, Ellis." "Trust God!"

I contacted all of my family and friends to personally thank them for being on Zoom that morning. Honestly, I thought about the naysayers in my family who thought I would spend time behind bars and told me I should take the original deal of 4 years in prison. I briefly thought about some people that I considered close friends who never checked on me during the entire ordeal to see if I needed anything. I knew better than to let these intrusive thoughts enter my mind, but for a moment, I had to remind myself who was real and who was fake. Ultimately, it didn't matter what they thought of me; it was a personal test of my faith in God, who, in the end, gets all the Glory for this victory.

Our bags were packed, and once again, a week later, we were on our way to Georgia for my graduation ceremony. A ceremony that felt more like a moment that stood still in time. I was proud of myself, but it wasn't the same feeling I got when Chris graduated. I knew that this accomplishment meant so much to many of us. The sacrifices that were made to get to this very moment could be huge for some graduates, but I felt no one sacrificed more than me. I studied so hard to get the grades worthy of bragging rights. There was a different drive behind it, however. I was Black. I mean, I knew that before, but I comprehend it differently now. I was Black in America, and after that nefarious act he committed, everything I pursued, I felt the need to attach perfection to it in order to be accepted and not rejected. I'm far from a psychologist, but trauma can cause a shift in your thinking indefinitely that, if not carefully rewired and reprogrammed, can cause you to never rise from the ashes of your torment.

It was my turn to have my name called to accept my degree. This was my moment in time that signified I was a Master in my field of education. As I walked up on stage and investigated the crowd, I instantly went into a trance-like state where the Dean looked at me concerned and said,

"Young man, are you okay?" I snapped out of it, smiled, and said, "Yes, I'm okay!" We shook hands, and out of nowhere, I raised both my hands as I walked across the stage like the Champ I was and relished the moment. In my language of origin, I began to say, "Mwen se yon chanpyonm mesi Bondye mwen rive!" I'm a champion; thank God, I made it!" I got what I worked so hard to obtain in life despite the heavy burdens that, like arrows, were attacking me from every direction. I had my hammer and nails ready to place my degree in a frame and hang it on the Wall of Fame.

After the ceremony, my family and I were so happy that in the parking lot, I felt compelled to testify on camera that I was not your average individual. I wanted all to know that I had done the impossible with the support of my family and friends, of course, God the Father. I was standing in front of my car with my cap and gown on, with my son standing right behind me. Laura had her camera phone out and hit record, and I began to thank everybody who had my back throughout this ordeal. Max, Waiguy, my brothers and sisters, my in-laws, The Beast, and anyone I could think of on the spot. I was reminded of Paul and Silas, who were thrown in prison and prayed earnestly to God to see them out of their despair. (Acts 16) When you make up in your mind that no matter the circumstance, good or bad, you must believe that your life story would be used as an example to inspire and uplift a person in this life. I persevered in the best way I knew how to honor my deceased parents, whose beliefs and morals I believed in so strongly. Morals that I have handed down to my children because doing the right thing matters in life. I released so many emotions of gratitude and self-happiness that I started stuttering while Laura was recording. I lost my words, but my heart was pure and so full of gratitude, knowing that I defeated all odds that were against me.

CHAPTER 22
HOPE FOR TOMORROW

I began my community service right away, cleaning up garbage alongside other men who were on probation. I must say that I was enlightened to learn a little about the lives of the other men because we were different, but there was something we all had in common that caused us to be there, and that was breaking the law. The law was the law, whether your punishment was valid or not, and I chose to make the best of the situation.

About a month after the court date, The Beast was able to file a motion for me to regain certain driving privileges, and I was granted the right to drive my car to church, doctor's appointments, to search for work, and, of course, to see my probation officer and my lawyer. That was another huge win for me, as the path to redemption doesn't happen all at once, the way destruction does.

Five years later, I am still being rejected at every job interview to be an educator. I sat in Zoom interviews and even interviewed in person, hoping to begin my career as an educator. I possessed all the credentials and certainly had the passion behind it. With any teaching position, a background check is required, and with a felony on my record comes the denial. In one of my interviews, I was upfront with my potential employer and expounded upon the reason I had a felony on my record because I believed that being transparent would help me earn points, but the interview didn't go any further. Once again, in the state of Florida, you are restricted from obtaining work in certain fields if you're a felon. It's so disheartening to hear the constant rejection from employers, and it stabs at the wounds of my past that I'm trying to heal from. My wife, Laura, is still carrying the weight of the bills, as I'm using my skills as an audio-visual tech to bring in money to help.

I was compelled to tell my story as an outlet to fulfill my purpose of uplifting and reaching the youth positively in some way. As of now, I'm being blocked from teaching in the school systems, so I pray this short story of depravity and redemption can touch the hearts and minds of the reader in two ways. One, I pray that if you've ever had a dream of becoming a better version of yourself, and life hits you with the worst of scenarios, you never give up on your dream. Because if you can see it, it will happen. Two, I pray that if you feel something tugging at your spirit to change your negative behaviors, you act upon it swiftly. It is a warning that what you do can have a tremendous negative impact affecting yourself and innocent people. Although the "Bad Guy" is resting in his grave, I feel as if I've been buried alive, fighting each day to continue on my journey in this life.

I am patiently waiting for God to grant me favor again so I can live out my dream as an educator in the classroom. I want to share one last detail that can be used as an example of what it truly means to "Keep your Eyes on the Prize."

My wife always puts everyone first, and when it's time to pour into herself, she's always running on fumes. On January 12, 2024, a FedEx envelope came in the mail, holding Laura's Bachelor's degree in Information Technology from the University of Phoenix. She had accomplished her goal of obtaining her degree after starting and stopping over a long period of time. There was a letter from the dean with a header that read, BE FEARLESS IN THE PURSUIT OF YOUR GOALS. Her ability to cope with burden after burden and still tackle her goals with such tenacity simply amazed me. She walked across the stage in Detroit, Michigan, with her peers. The whole family came out to support her because, in the words of Langston Hughes, "life for me ain't been no crystal stair." We all have benefited from having Laura in our lives in some way, shape, or form. She may feel like she comes last to everybody, but I know God says the first shall be last, and the last shall be first. She is the real MVP. Our Wall of Fame is complete until further notice.

ΛCKNOWLEDGMENTS

I want to thank everyone who encouraged me through my darkest moments. A special thanks to those who were there to encourage me, even when things weren't going right in my life. Without your love and support, this would not have been possible. Becoming a writer requires a lot of thinking and dedication. I have come to realize that a strong support system makes the impossible possible. To the Pierre Louis Family, I will never forget you. I cannot describe how thankful I am for the love and kindness you have bestowed upon me; I want to express a special thank you.

To the Newell family, words cannot express the amount of gratitude and appreciation I have for you all. To my bonus Mother Pamela, whom I love as dearly as my own mother, Queen, your spiritual and mental support was key in my time of need. I love you so much.

MEET ELLIS GEORGES

Ellis Georges is a family man who has become the first of his generation to receive a master's degree in education. As a first-time author, Ellis has proven his resilience by penning this story to inspire others to never give up on themselves. His love for God, family, and the willingness to stand up for what he believes in has lifted the spirits of hundreds of people. Ellis resides in Miami, FL, and enjoys spending quality time with his family.

Email: imellisgeorges@gmail.com

instagram.com/Iamellisgeorges

tiktok.com/@iamellisgeorge

youtube.com/@IamEllisGeorgesTV

MEET BLESSING WELLS

Blessing Wells is a passionate entrepreneur and first-time co-author based in Las Vegas, NV, where she has spent the last three years successfully running her salon. As a devoted wife and mother of three kids, Blessing thrives on helping others discover their best selves, using storytelling as a powerful tool to inspire those around her. With God at the center of her life, she demonstrates the importance of following one's passion while nurturing relationships and staying grounded in faith.

Email:Authorblessingwells@outlook.com

instagram.com/AuthorBlessingWells